Self-Awareness

THE SCHOOL OF LIFE
Essential Ideas

Self-Awareness

Published in 2024 by The School of Life
First published in the USA in 2024
930 High Road, London, N12 9RT

Copyright © The School of Life 2024

Designed and typeset by Myfanwy Vernon-Hunt
Printed in China by Leo Paper Group

A proportion of this book has appeared online at
www.theschooloflife.com/articles

Every effort has been made to contact the copyright holders
of the material reproduced in this book. If any have been
inadvertently overlooked, the publisher will be pleased to
make restitution at the earliest opportunity.

The School of Life publishes a range of books on essential topics
in psychological and emotional life, including relationships,
parenting, friendship, careers and fulfilment. The aim is always
to help us to understand ourselves better – and thereby to
grow calmer, less confused and more purposeful. Discover
our full range of titles, including books for children, here:
www.theschooloflife.com/books

The School of Life also offers a comprehensive therapy service,
which complements, and draws upon, our published works:
www.theschooloflife.com/therapy

www.theschooloflife.com

ISBN 978-1-916753-02-0

10 9 8 7 6 5 4 3 2 1

Contents

Introduction

Socrates, the earliest and greatest of philosophers, summed up the purpose of philosophy in one resonant phrase: 'know yourself'. A capacity for self-awareness is at the heart of our inclinations to forgiveness, kindness, creativity and wise decision-making, especially around love and work. Unfortunately, knowing ourselves is the (always unfinished) task of a lifetime. We are permanently elusive and mysterious to ourselves.

Self-awareness might be said to involve a set of fundamental realisations about the relationship between past and present.

– Who we are today is, to a humbling and maddening degree, the result of events and dynamics in childhood we cannot for the most part remember, almost certainly don't seek to explore and are understandably invested in trying to think well of.

– Most of our difficulties come down to a shortfall in love in childhood. The physical vulnerability of children has its counterpart in an elevated degree of emotional susceptibility. Not very much needs to have happened in order for us to pick up a substantial wound.

– We spend a great deal of energy in trying not to understand our pasts, in the name of maintaining our poise, our illusions and our self-respect. Most of who we are lies in the unconscious.

– What we feel will happen next around people in general carries complex echoes of what happened back then around certain people in particular. With great unfairness, we constantly attribute to people in the here and now motives and likely patterns of behaviour unknowingly derived from figures from our histories.

– We become slightly less difficult to be around when we start to appreciate the extent to which we are continually distorting reality through lenses scratched by our pasts. Maturity means no longer insisting too hard on our sanity.

– To go back over the past is almost certainly going to be a mixture of frightening and irritating. It would be extremely odd if we didn't have very mixed feelings about the business of self-examination.

One of the tasks of culture is to offer us tools to assist us with the task of self-awareness. We need a vocabulary to name feelings and states of mind; we need encouragement to be alone with ourselves at regular moments; we need friends and professionals who will listen to us with sympathy and we need works of art that can illuminate elusive aspects of our psyches.

Above all, we need to be modest about our capacity to easily understand who we are and what we want. We should nurture a stance of scepticism towards many of our first impulses and submit all our significant plans to extensive rational cross-examination.

Failures of self-awareness lie behind some of our gravest individual and collective disasters.

What follows is 25 ideas on self-awareness that will set us on the path to truly understanding ourselves.

Akrasia

A central problem of our minds is that we know so much in theory about how we should behave but engage so little with our knowledge in our day-to-day conduct.

We know in theory about not eating too much, being kind, getting to bed early, focusing on our opportunities before it is too late, showing charity and remembering to be grateful. Yet in practice, our wise ideas have a notoriously weak ability to motivate our actual behaviour. Our knowledge is embedded within us and yet is ineffective for us.

The Ancient Greeks were unusually alert to this phenomenon and gave it a helpfully resonant name: *akrasia*, commonly translated as 'weakness of will'. It is because of akrasia, they proposed, that we have such a tragic proclivity for knowing what to do but not acting upon our own best principles.

There are two central solutions to akrasia, located in two unexpected quarters: art and ritual. The real purpose of art (which includes novels, films and songs as well as photos, paintings and works of design and architecture) is to give emotional lustre to a range of ideas that are most important to us, but that are also most under threat in the conditions of everyday life. Art shouldn't be a matter of introducing us to, or challenging us with, a stream of new ideas so much as about lending the good ideas we already have compelling forms – so that they can more readily weigh upon our behaviour. A euphoric song should activate the reserves of tenderness in which we already believe in theory; a novel should move us to the forgiveness in which we are already invested at an intellectual level.

Ritual is the second defence we have against akrasia. By ritual, we mean the structured, often highly seductive or aesthetic, repetition of a thought or an action, with a view to making it at once convincing and habitual. Our brains are leaky, and under pressure of any kind, readily revert to customary patterns of thought and feeling. Ritual trains our cognitive muscles; it makes a sequence of appointments in our diaries to refresh our acquaintance with our most important ideas.

Our current culture tends to see ritual mainly as an antiquated infringement of individual freedom; a bossy command to turn our thoughts in particular directions at specific times. But the defenders of ritual would see it another way: we aren't being told to think of something we don't agree with; we are being returned with grace to what we always believed in at heart.

The greatest human institutions that have tried to address the problem of akrasia have been religions. Religions have wanted to do something much more serious than simply promote abstract ideas: they have wanted to get people to behave in line with those ideas. They didn't just want people to think that kindness or forgiveness were nice (which we generally do already); they wanted us to be kind or forgiving most days of the year. They invented a host of ingenious mechanisms for mobilising the will, which is why, across much of the world, the finest art and buildings, the most seductive music, the most impressive and moving rituals have all been religious.

This has presented a conundrum for a more secular era. Bad secularisation has lumped together religious superstition and religion's anti-akrasia strategies. It has rejected both the supernatural ideas of the faiths and their wise attitude to the motivational roles of art and ritual.

A more discerning form of secularisation makes a major distinction between (on the one hand) religion as a set of speculative claims about God and (on the other hand) the always valid ambition to improve our psychological lives by combatting our notoriously weak wills.

The challenge for the secular world is now to redevelop its own versions of purposeful art and ritual so that we will cease so regularly to ignore our real commitments and might henceforth not only believe wise things but also, on a day-to-day basis, have a slightly higher chance of enacting wisdom in our lives.

Anxiety

Anxiety is not a sign of sickness, a weakness of the mind or an error to which we should always locate a medical solution. It is mostly a reasonable and sensitive response to the genuine strangeness, terror, uncertainty and riskiness of existence.

Anxiety is our fundamental state for well-founded reasons: because we are intensely vulnerable physical beings, a complicated network of fragile organs biding their time before letting us down catastrophically at a moment of their own choosing. Because we have insufficient information upon which to make most major life decisions. Because we can imagine so much more than we have and live in ambitious mediatised societies where envy and restlessness are constant. Because we are the descendants of the great worriers of the species, the others having been torn apart by wild animals, and because we still carry in our DNA – into the calm of the suburbs – the terrors of the savannah. Because our careers play out within the tough-minded, competitive, destructive, random workings of an uncontained economic engine. Because we rely for our self-esteem on the love of people we cannot control and whose needs and hopes will never align seamlessly with our own.

All of which is not to say that there aren't better and worse ways to approach our condition. The single most important move is acceptance. There is no need to be anxious that we are anxious on top of everything else. The mood is no sign that our lives have gone wrong; merely that we are alive. We should also be more careful when pursuing things we imagine will spare us anxiety. We can head to them by all means, but for other reasons than fantasies of calm – and with a little less vigour and a little more scepticism. We will still be anxious when we finally have the house, the love affair and the right income.

We should spare ourselves the burden of loneliness. We are far from the only ones with this problem. Everyone is more anxious than they are inclined to tell us. Even the tycoon and the couple in love are suffering. We have collectively failed to admit to ourselves how much we panic.

We must learn to laugh about our anxieties – laughter being the exuberant expression of relief when a hitherto private agony is given a well-crafted social formulation in a joke. We must suffer alone. But we can at least hold out our arms to our similarly tortured, fractured and anxious neighbours, as if to say, in the kindest way possible: 'I know...'

Anxiety deserves greater dignity. It is not a sign of degeneracy. It is a kind of masterpiece of insight: a justifiable expression of our mysterious participation in a disordered, uncertain world.

Being 'Good'

We tend to assume that all is well with good children. They don't pose immediate problems; they keep their bedroom tidy, do their homework on time and are willing to help with the washing up. But the very real secret sorrows – and future difficulties – of the good child are tied to the fact that they behave in this way not out of choice, but because they feel under irresistible pressure to do so. They are trying to cope with adults who project the idea that only the ideally compliant child is truly loveable.

As a result, the good child becomes an expert at pleasing their audience, while their real thoughts and feelings stay buried. Eventually, under pressure, these good children may manifest some disturbing symptoms: secret sulphurous bitterness, sudden outbursts of rage and very harsh views of their own imperfections.

The good person typically has particular problems around sex. As a child, they may have been praised for being pure and innocent. As an adult the most exciting parts of their own sexuality strike them as perverse, disgusting and deeply at odds with who they are meant to be. As an adult, the good child is likely to have problems at work as well. They feel too strong a need to follow the rules, never make trouble or annoy anyone. But almost everything that is interesting or worth doing will meet with a degree of opposition and will seriously irritate some people. The good child is condemned to career mediocrity and people-pleasing.

The desire to be good is one of the loveliest things in the world, but in order to have a genuinely good life, we may sometimes need to be (by the standards of the good child) fruitfully and bravely bad.

Confidence

Although we assume that we must want to be confident, in our hearts, we may harbour suspicions that confidence is in fact an unappealing state of mind. Without fully realising it, we might find the idea of being truly confident strangely offensive, and secretly remain attached to hesitancy and modesty.

Suspicion of confidence has traditionally enjoyed immense cultural endorsement. Christianity – for centuries the greatest influence on the mindset of the West – was highly sceptical about those who think too well of themselves. While the meek basked in divine favour, the arrogant would be the last to enter the kingdom of heaven. The political theory of Karl Marx added to this argument a set of ideas apparently proving that economic success was founded upon the exploitation of others. No wonder it may feel as if – to be moral citizens – we should steer clear of all overly robust assertions of our own interests.

Yet this attitude too can carry dangers. We may lack the confidence not to be cruel and promote greed, but to fight for kindness and wisdom. Our lack of confidence in confidence may be allowing degraded versions of self-assertion to thrive.

Maybe we are just being unfair. Our negative view of confidence can be overly dependent on the quirks of our own histories, or on the sort of people in whom we first encountered confidence, who were not its best representatives. Our real problem may not be confidence so much as a lack of other virtues such as manners, charm and generosity. We may be wrongly diagnosing the root of our objections. There may be a danger of growing into braggarts and self-seekers. But confidence is in its essence compatible with remaining sensitive, kind and softly spoken. It might be brutishness, not confidence, that we hate.

Furthermore, our attraction to meekness may mask some rather cowardly resentments against self-assertion. We might not so much admire timidity as fear giving confidence a try. It was this species of self-protective deception that particularly fascinated the philosopher Nietzsche. He thought it a typical error of many Christians, who might pride themselves on their 'forgiveness' while simply trying to excuse their 'inability to take revenge'. We should take care not to dress up our base deficiencies as godly virtues.

Unfortunately, it isn't enough to be kind, interesting, intelligent and wise inside: we need to develop the skill that allows us to make our talents active in the world at large. Confidence is what translates theory into practice. It should never be thought of as the enemy of good things; it is their crucial and legitimate catalyst. We should allow ourselves to develop confidence in confidence.

Conscience

It's one of the quirks of our brains that we don't notice as sharply as we might when we move from one area of their functioning to another. Our thoughts about wanting to eat a sandwich, reflecting on the meaning of love, moving our left elbow away from the radiator, or repairing a relationship with a friend flow in a single seamless uninterrupted sequence, even though our thoughts will have originated in quite different regions of the brain, with their own evolutionary histories, priorities and drives.

Part of this neglect for the varied origins of thoughts means we seldom notice when a distinct part of our minds takes command that we call our conscience. It's our conscience that directs what flows through consciousness when we are five minutes late for a meeting and chide ourselves for not having left the house earlier. Or when we realise we forgot to answer a message from a colleague or when we note, at midday, that we are far behind on the goals we had set ourselves for the day. It's our conscience that is home to our guilt, shame and self-criticism.

We might have been on the earth a long while before we become aware – perhaps under the prompting of a kind friend or an observant therapist – exactly how stern, and at moments even plain violent, our conscience seems to be. We're not only a bit embarrassed to be late for the meeting, we're a damn idiot for messing up again. We're not only somewhat ashamed for how we performed at work, we're a disgrace who never gets ourself together.

Once we realise we have a conscience and that it speaks to us in a very partial manner, we are in a better position to reflect on the issue of its origins. To compress the matter: the way we speak to ourselves is an internalisation of the way others once spoke to us. Our conscience has been formed from the voices of our earliest caregivers.

The thesis opens up an opportunity for questions. Do we like the way we speak to ourselves when we are late? Do we think it's useful to treat ourselves as we do when we have been rejected in love? And more broadly, how do we feel about the people who taught us about right and wrong, about guilt and duty, about effort and necessity?

Our conscience may be speaking to us in voices far removed from the values we otherwise esteem. If we saw someone else treating a stranger the way we treat ourselves, would we be impressed?

It may be time to disentangle the voices of the figures of our pasts from the gentler, more productive attitudes we long for and hold dear at an intellectual level. We can build ourselves the conscience we would want for a child or a friend we love.

Defensiveness

The trait we should perhaps be keenest to vanquish in any attempt to become a proper emotional grown-up is defensiveness – a pattern of response that lies behind more broken relationships, distraught families and dysfunctional workplaces than any other.

What defines the defensive person is their recourse to demoralising aggression, denial and irritation in the face of unwelcome pieces of information about their character. Sometimes, what we are trying to tell them will be discounted on the basis that we ourselves are not invariably without fault – and therefore that we have no right to try to improve anyone else (neatly missing that we only have insight into the fragilities of others because we are not personally beyond reproach). Or else our remarks will be undermined by a cynicism as to our motives: we might be told that we are jealous or inadequate, anything other than the more troubling notion that we might be trying to share an insight because we care.

We need to start with an understanding of the true cause and underlying fuel of defensiveness, namely, self-ignorance. We flare up in response to the comments of others because we are operating, deep down, with an unclear picture of who we are. We are angry because we have no reliable map of our virtues and vices, because we are oscillating between a brittle faith in our accomplishments and a bleak terror of our flaws.

The self-aware person has overcome any such uncertainty. They will long ago have exchanged perfectionism and self-loathing for a more stable and judicious assessment of their natures, as much in their positive as in their negative dimensions. There will be nothing that their worst enemy can tell them that they have not – with realism – either bravely taken on board or serenely rejected already.

Some of what they have recognised will be truly sombre: yes, they really are quite silly. Unfortunately, they truly are very bad in bed. Lamentably, they haven't necessarily been a good parent. But these ideas are now well-known, they have been raked over and digested, there isn't any need to insist spitefully or nervously on their opposites.

At the same time, self-knowledge sets useful limits on how much we need to despise ourselves. The self-aware explorer will recognise that they are imperfect in many ways, but they will also know that they genuinely aren't wholly monstrous either.

We will be past defensiveness when every nagging insecurity that we had previously banished to the periphery of consciousness has been pulled squarely into the centre and there examined and defused. Thereafter, we might hear much that is negative, but we'll never need to bite in response to a remark, because either it will be false, and therefore can be discarded without fluster. Or else it will be true, and we'll be able to remain even-tempered because we'll be as aware as our angriest opponent of its justice and validity. We'll know who we are – and so will never need to greet a challenging idea about us with weapons again.

Emotional
Education

We accept a major role for education at the centre of our societies. We invest in ensuring that knowledge built up in one generation can be reliably transferred to another.

However, our Romantic culture places a curious limit around the idea of what can fairly be taught and transferred. We know that we can teach people how to fly a plane, perform brain surgery or analyse the tax returns of medium-sized businesses – and a host of institutions exist to carry out instruction in these fields.

However, it would sound distinctly odd to imagine that we might learn, for example, how to love someone, how to become wise, how to grow less agitated, or how to die well. Our Romantic culture assumes that in these fields, we are simply more or less born knowing how to live, and that there is precious little that one human could ever systematically teach another.

Emotional education is the term given to the contrary belief that we can and must train ourselves in our emotional conduct. We should, its adherents propose, be schooled to respond in more equitable and intelligent ways to our impulses, desires and fears. Emotions are not fixed, unchangeable or reliable tendencies. We can learn how to be more forgiving; how to extend the range of our sympathies; how to grow more confident, accepting and self-aware.

It is because we have – until now – not taken emotional education seriously enough that our species has grown ever more technically adept while retaining the level of wisdom of our earliest days, with catastrophic results. It appears that the fate of civilisation now depends on our capacity to master the mechanisms of emotional education before it is too late.

Emotional education extends far beyond formal education as we have conceived of it to date. Although it should ideally include specialised courses in every year of school, emotional education is more than something that should take place in classrooms at the hands of teachers and come to a halt around the age of 21.

The central vehicle for the transfer of emotional intelligence is culture, from its highest to its most popular level. Culture is the field that can ritualise and promote the absorption of wisdom. The 'lessons' of culture might be embedded in a TV series, a pop song or a novel. We can envisage the entire apparatus of culture as a subtle mechanism designed to point us towards greater wisdom.

We will never progress as a species, and will indeed grow into ever-greater technologically armed menaces to ourselves, until we have accepted the challenges and opportunities of emotional education.

Emotional
Intelligence

Emotional intelligence is the quality that enables us to confront with patience, insight and imagination the many problems that we face in our affective relationship with ourselves and with others.

The term may sound odd. We are used to referring to intelligence as a general quality, without unpicking a particular variety that a person might possess; therefore, we do not tend to highlight the value of a distinctive sort of intelligence that currently does not enjoy the prestige it should.

Every sort of intelligence signals an ability to navigate well around a particular set of challenges: mathematical, linguistic, technical, commercial. When we say that someone is clever but has messed up their personal life, or that they have acquired a fortune but are restless and sad, or that they are powerful but intolerant and unimaginative, we are pointing to a deficit in emotional intelligence.

In social life, we can feel the presence of emotional intelligence in a sensitivity to the moods of others and in a readiness to grasp the surprising things that may be going on for them beneath the surface. Emotional intelligence recognises a role for interpretation and knows that a fiery outburst might be a disguised plea, or that concealed within a forceful jolliness may be a sorrow that has been sentimentally disavowed.

In relation to ourselves, emotional intelligence shows up in a scepticism around our emotions, especially those of love, desire, anger, envy, anxiety and professional ambition. The emotionally intelligent refuse to trust their first impulses or the wisdom of their feelings. They know that hatred may mask love, that anger may be a cover for sadness, and that we are prone to huge and costly inaccuracies in whom we desire and what we seek.

Emotional intelligence is also what distinguishes those who are crushed by failure from those who can greet the troubles of existence with a melancholy and at points darkly humorous resilience. The emotionally intelligent appreciate the role of well-handled pessimism within the overall economy of a good life.

Emotional intelligence is not an inborn talent. It is the result of education – specifically in how to interpret ourselves, where our emotions arise from, how our childhoods influence us and how we might best navigate our fears and wishes.

Our technical intelligence has led us to tame nature and conquer the planet. A wiser, saner future for the race will depend on our capacity to master and then seductively teach the rudiments of emotional intelligence – while there is still time.

Emotional
Scepticism

Emotional scepticism refers to an attitude of good-natured suspicion towards the majority of our first impulses and feelings. The emotional sceptic rarely fully trusts what they immediately desire, what they fear and what their so-called 'gut' tells them. They understand their minds to be 'faulty walnuts', highly liable to be throwing off inaccurate or misleading emotions. They like to pause and create a 'fireguard' between their feelings and their actions.

Emotional sceptics will take their time coming to decisions. They sleep on things. They don't simply act on impulse. They are disinclined to get married after two exceptionally glorious weeks.

Our current culture looks askance at emotional scepticism. It sounds very boring, sexless and unimpressive. We are still guided by the Romantic notion that emotions are the voices of our true selves, requiring to be honoured as faithfully and as quickly as possible.

This background ideology explains why there is still so much folly at large – and why emotional scepticism is such a priority.

Eudaimonia

Eudaimonia is an Ancient Greek word, particularly emphasised by the philosophers Plato and Aristotle, that deserves wider currency. It corrects the shortfalls in one of the most central, governing but insufficient terms in our contemporary idiom: *happiness*.

When we nowadays try to articulate the purpose of our lives, it is to the word 'happiness' that we commonly have recourse. We tell ourselves and others that the ultimate rationale for our jobs, our relationships and the conduct of our day-to-day lives is the pursuit of happiness. It sounds like an innocent enough idea, but excessive reliance on the term means that we are frequently unfairly tempted to exit or at least heavily question a great many testing but worthwhile situations.

The Ancient Greeks resolutely did not believe that the purpose of life was to be happy; they proposed that it was to achieve eudaimonia, a word that has been best translated as 'fulfilment'.

What distinguishes happiness from fulfilment is pain. It is eminently possible to be fulfilled and, at the same time, under pressure, suffering physically or mentally, overburdened and frequently tetchy. This is a psychological nuance that the word 'happiness' makes it hard to capture, for it is tricky to speak of being happy yet suffering. However, such a combination is readily accommodated within the dignified and noble-sounding letters of eudaimonia.

The word encourages us to trust that many of life's most worthwhile projects will at points be quite at odds with contentment and yet are worth pursuing, nevertheless. Properly exploring our professional talents, managing a household, keeping a relationship going, creating a new business venture – none of these goals is likely to leave us cheerful and grinning on a quotidian basis. They will involve us in all manner of challenges that will exhaust us, provoke and wound us. Yet we will, perhaps, at the end of our lives, still feel that the tasks were worth undertaking. Through them, we will have accessed something grander and more interesting than happiness: we will have made a difference.

With the word eudaimonia in mind, we can stop imagining that we should aim for a pain-free existence, and then berate ourselves unfairly for being in a bad mood. We will know that we are trying to do something far more important than smile: we are striving to do justice to our full human potential and to work in some key way towards the improvement of our species.

Good Enough

The mid-20th-century psychoanalyst, Donald Winnicott, who specialised in working with parents and children, was disturbed by how often he encountered in his consulting rooms parents who were deeply disappointed with themselves. They felt they were failing as parents and hated themselves intensely as a result. They were ashamed of their occasional rows, their bursts of short temper, their times of boredom around their own children and their many mistakes. They were haunted by a range of anxious questions: are we too strict, too lenient, too protective, not protective enough? What struck Winnicott, however, was that these people were almost always not at all bad parents. They were loving, often very kind, and very interested in their children; they tried hard to meet their needs and to understand their problems as best they could. As parents they were – as he came to put it in a hugely memorable and important phrase – 'good enough'.

Winnicott identified a crucial issue. We often torment ourselves because we have in our minds a very demanding, and in fact impossible, vision of what we're supposed to be like across a range of areas of our lives. This vision doesn't emerge from a careful study of what actual people are like; it's a fantasy, a punitive perfectionism, drawn from the cultural ether.

When it comes to parenting, we imagine a fantasy of parents who are always calm, always perfectly wise, always there when their child needs them. There are no parents like this. But a Romantic conception of the perfect parent can fill our minds and make us deeply anxious because our own family life inevitably looks so messy and muddled by comparison. Unreasonably inflated expectations leave us only able to perceive where we have fallen short.

With the phrase 'good enough', Winnicott was initiating a hugely important project. He wanted to move us away from idealisation. Ideals may sound nice, but they bring a terrible problem in their wake: they can make us despair of the merely quite good things we already do and have. 'Good enough' is a cure for the sickness of idealisation.

Winnicott introduced the idea of 'good enough' around parenting, but it applies widely across our lives. For example, we might refer to the 'good enough' job. It may not meet our fantasy demands: creative yet secure; fascinating but not stressful. But by the standards of what real jobs are like, it might be worth taking pride in. Or we could speak of the 'good enough' marriage. It might not be the perfect union of two souls, sex may be intermittent, there may be regular frustrations. But by the standards of actual long-term relationships, that might be genuine success.

By dialling down our expectations, the idea of 'good enough' re-sensitises us to the lesser, but very real, virtues we already possess, but that our unreal hopes have made us overlook.

A 'good enough' life is not a bad life. It's the best existence that humans are ever likely to lead.

Inner Idiot

The 'inner idiot' is a bracing term used to describe a substantial, hugely influential and strenuously concealed part of everyone. An idiot is what we deeply fear being; it is what we suspect in our darkest hours that we might be; and it is what we should simply accept, with humour and good grace, that we often truly are. A decent life isn't one in which we foolishly believe we can slay or evade the inner idiot; it's one in which we practise the only art available to us: sensible cohabitation.

The inner idiot makes itself felt at moments small and large. The idiot is clumsy: it forgets names, loses important documents, spills food down its front and gets air kisses wrong. The idiot is prickly, it gets into rages because it was momentarily ignored, it sees plots against it where there were only accidents and is immediately self-righteous when faced with the most minor criticism. It is, for the idiot, always someone else's fault. The inner idiot is a child on a bad day.

We know our own inner idiot from the inside and might suppose it is unique to us. In fact, it represents what might be called the 'lower' self of all of humanity. It is only residual good manners that has made the inner idiot of others less obvious to us – and hence made our own seem like a freakish exception.

There is wisdom in accepting that the inner idiot will never go away and that we should therefore endeavour to form a good working relationship with it.

Trying to prevent the emergence of the inner idiot otherwise inspires a range of unfortunate traits. For example, we may lose confidence and grow unnecessarily meek and cautious in a bid to appear dignified and serious in front of others. We may refuse ever to ask someone for a date or for a pay rise; we might never go travelling on our own or give a speech in public, as all of these moves require a calculated risk of being hijacked by the idiot.

By denying our idiot, we may grow unfeasibly pompous and stiff. Nothing makes us seem absurd faster than insisting on our own seriousness. We are always better off confessing to idiocy in good time, rather than letting it emerge from behind our carefully constructed pretensions.

By squaring up to the existence of the inner idiot, we may come to feel a useful compassion for ourselves. Of course we made a mess of certain things; of course we made some bad decisions; of course we said the wrong things. What else could we have done, given that we are hosting a powerfully idiotic being in our minds and that our rational cleverness and goodness sit precariously on top of its many deeply unintelligent impulses?

We may spread our compassion to others as well. They were not necessarily evil when they hurt us; they merely possess a domineering idiot of their own.

The best school for learning about the inner idiot is comedy. The essence of comedy is to expose the workings of the idiot in a way that invites sympathetic laughter rather than harsh criticism.

Love is another solution to the problems of the inner idiot. In its most mature and desired sense, love means encountering and embracing the idiot of another, regarding it not with horror or as an affront, but with all the imagination and generosity with which a parent might look upon their beloved 2-year-old in a tantrum.

A wise society would be ambitious about understanding, accommodating and forgiving the inner idiot in everyone, and would be devoted to finding ways to soothe it and limit its influence.

It is one of the greatest of all human achievements when we can finally move from seeing someone as an 'idiot' to being able to consider them as that far less offensive and more morally hybrid creature: a 'loveable idiot'.

Inner Voices

We all have inner voices in our minds. They talk to us as we try to achieve things or deal with our lives. Sometimes they are kind, but often they are punitive, telling us we're stupid or worthless or that we deserve every misfortune that comes our way.

An inner voice was always once an outer voice that we have imperceptibly made our own. Perhaps we have absorbed the tone of a harassed or angry parent; the menacing threats of an elder sibling keen to put us down; the contempt of a schoolyard bully, or the words of a teacher who seemed impossible to please. We take in these voices because, at certain key moments in the past, they sounded compelling and irresistible. The dominant figures of our individual histories repeated their messages over and over until they became lodged in our own way of thinking – sometimes to our great cost.

The ideal inner voice doesn't pretend that everything we do is wonderful. Rather, it is like the voice of an ideal friend. These figures can recognise when we have done something unwise, but they are merciful, fair, accurate in understanding what's going on and interested in helping us deal with our problems. It's not that we should stop judging ourselves; the hope is that we can learn to be better judges of ourselves.

Instead of promoting a self-flagellating critical internal commentary, a good friend represents a calm, constructive way of addressing failings.

Culture has a role to play here. If our surrounding culture is broadcasting voices that are at once realistic and supportive, complex and morally perceptive, it will be much easier for us to adopt this manner internally as we comment on the trickier parts of our own lives. External generous wisdom can take up residence in the place it is most needed: our private running conversation with ourselves.

Insomnia

Not being able to sleep is deeply frightening. We panic about our ability to cope with the demands of the next day. We panic that we are panicking. The possibility of sleep recedes ever further as the clock counts down to another exhausted, irritable dawn.

Insomnia is seldom a disease: it is an inarticulate, maddening but ultimately almost logical plea released by our core self, asking us to confront certain issues we've put off for too long. Insomnia isn't really to do with not being able to sleep; it's about not having given ourselves a chance to think. It is the revenge of all the many thoughts we didn't take seriously enough in the day.

Most of us do of course have a great deal on our minds during the daylight hours, but these tend to be practical, procedural, immediate matters – the sort that keep at bay the larger, deeper questions about our direction, purpose and values.

So important are some of the questions we need to tackle, something within us – you might call it an inner guardian or conscience – prefers that we should stop deriving all the many obvious benefits of sleep rather than leave a raft of existential issues untreated for much longer.

This points us towards a solution to insomnia: not so much a pill or a special kind of tea or a long bath, but,

principally, more time – in the reasonable hours of the day –
for thinking. More time in which there are no demands
upon us, and we can at last meditate philosophically – that
is, systematically examine everything we are concerned
about, sift through our regrets, discuss our work with our
inner critic, air the tensions of our relationship with our
true selves. In short, reacquaint ourselves with ourselves.

Mechanisms
of Defence

Getting to know ourselves better sounds, on the surface, like a project we might all buy into. But this is to underestimate the extent to which we are, just below the surface, typically highly invested in not getting to know or feel a range of important but troubling things about who we are. Whatever lip service we may pay to the project of self-awareness, we would – it seems – very much like not to know a great deal about our identities.

In order to shield us from ourselves, we rely on techniques known as 'mechanisms of defence': a range of astonishingly clever internal manoeuvres that subtly enable us to expel uncomfortable ideas from awareness without alerting our conscience and so return us to a blind placid equilibrium. It is thanks to these mechanisms of defence that we're able to convince ourselves that we hate someone we're actually drawn to (but can't have) or that we get depressed in lieu of getting angry with a person who has done us wrong but who we want to believe is good.

However effective they may be, mechanisms of defence ultimately impose a great psychic cost on us; they tie up our energies repressing ideas on which our growth relies. Our defences buy us short-term calm at the expense of long-term development.

A list of our mechanisms of defence might include the following:

The Grandiose Defence

Once upon a time, we felt catastrophically insignificant: we were humiliated and ignored by our caregivers and denied a basic sense that we had a right to exist. Many years later, grown and more capable, with arch rigidity, we make use of money, reputation and cultural capital to insist on a specialness that we can't – for that matter – ever truly believe in. We wield grandiosity as a shield against the risks of any renewed encounter with the neglected, powerless child still sobbing and forlorn somewhere inside us.

The Common-Sense Defence

We are filled with huge and painfully complicated truths; they might be about sexuality, love or money. There is so much that we might need to think about and would, as a result, need to mourn or grapple anxiously with. But we lack the courage and therefore settle on a highly consoling line of defence: that the whole field of psychology, the discipline that tries to draw our attention to ourselves, is 'psychobabble'. We dismiss its efforts as nonsense; we pride ourselves on calling a spade a spade and cling fervently to the solacing thought that our minds are lacking any of the complexity or folly that seems the universal lot.

The Manic Defence

We run strenuously from one project to another; we give ourselves no time at all to sit with our odder wishes and fears. It might have been a year since we last had a day without commitments. We devote manic energy to work, the news, exercise, to keep our unresolved thoughts at bay. The most terrifying prospect in the world might be to sit in silence with ourselves.

The Sadistic Defence

We choose to feel strong and in control by subjecting another to the pains we once endured as children. We make a colleague feel inept, we ensure our offspring knows how little they are worth, we criticise our partner for their countless departures from perfection. There are, in our deep minds, only two roles a person can play: victim or perpetrator. And we have firmly decided the one we'd rather be.

The Masochistic Defence

We feel too weak to prevent ourselves from suffering, but not too weak to turn our suffering into a sort of choice, even – in a manner of speaking – a kind of pleasure. So we actively search for partners who won't fulfil us, we criticise ourselves in the wake of every success, we gain a particular relish in being treated badly. We know we are going to suffer; but at least – this time around – we are in charge of inflicting the pain on ourselves.

Weaning ourselves from reliance on these mechanisms of defence is the work of a lifetime. Surrender of these mechanisms requires a leap of faith: that the price will eventually be worth it; that our symptoms will abate the more we understand them; that we will live more easily once we nurture the roots of self-awareness.

Mind and Body

The most curious and hazardous feature of the way we're built lies in the difficulty we have registering what we actually feel. Our vast and strange minds get filled with thoughts that go unsifted and with feelings we don't have the courage to look at. We might be angry or sad while lacking any active awareness that we are so. Or guilty or envious without any grasp of what is at play behind a thin psychological curtain. And we remain unconscious because we are resistant to ideas that threaten our sense of calm and our gratifying illusions about ourselves.

While the greatest share of our mental apparatus privileges forgetting over understanding, there's a part of us that wants the truth, however bitter it might be; a minor part, but a notoriously insistent part that won't leave us in peace until its case has been heard. It will, in order to stir us from our reverie, give us all manner of problems – breakdowns, illnesses, twitches, compulsions – in the hope of letting us know that there is something we would benefit from reckoning with.

When our conscience has done everything it can to alert our minds, it has a tendency to set to work on our bodies. More specifically, it forces us to feel in the form of a symptom what we haven't felt outright as an idea or insight. Lack of awareness returns to haunt us as physical ailments.

If our intellect won't look at our anger, the feeling may be sent to dwell in our lower back. If our anxiety isn't being dealt with psychologically, it may be relegated to our gut. Our unfelt feelings end up as back pain, constipation, migraines and arrhythmias.

In order to spare our bodies some of their mute agonies, we should submit them to a curious-sounding exercise. With our eyes closed, probably while we are lying in bed, we should pass over our different organs and zones and ask: If this could speak, what might it want to tell us? What might the heart ask for, the legs, the shoulders, the stomach?

Our minds are probably better able to think of answers than we presume. It could be surprisingly clear – once we ask the question – that our shoulders are desperate for the relationship to end; that our stomachs want us to take on less responsibility; that our hearts want a chance to say sorry and that our lungs need an opportunity to scream.

Many of our bodily ailments are ultimately mute forms of revenge for the thoughts and feelings we have assiduously been refusing to entertain. We will feel so much better in our bodies once we have repatriated our concerns to our minds; once we have dared to see and endure what we have been in flight from for too long.

News from
Within

To lay claim to any respectability or competence, we know that we must keep up with the news. That's why we've ringed the earth with satellites and created networks of bureaus that inform us with maniacal urgency of pretty much any event to have unfolded anywhere on the planet in the last few moments. Furthermore, we are equipped with tiny devices that we keep very close to hand, so as to monitor all unfolding stories in real time. We have been granted a ringside seat to the second-by-second flow of history.

As a result, we see a lot more. At the same time, strangely, we see a lot less. The constant presence of news from without hampers our ability to pick up on an equally important, though far less prestigious, source of news from within. We are not, by nature, well equipped to see inside ourselves. Consciousness bobs like a small boat on a sea of disavowed emotions. A lot of feelings and ideas require a high degree of courage to confront. They threaten to make us uncomfortably anxious, excited or sad were we to learn more about them.

So, we use the news from without to silence the news from within. We have the most prestigious excuse ever invented not to spend too much time roaming freely inside our own minds. It is not that the news from without is unimportant to someone – it will be the most important thing in certain people's lives a continent away, or in a company in the capital, or somewhere in the upper reaches of government. It's just that this news is almost certainly disconnected from our real priority over the coming years, which is to make the most of our life and our talents in the time that remains to us. It is touching that we should give so much of our curiosity over to strangers, but it is poignant that we are forced eventually to pay such a high price for this constant dispersal of energy. We dismiss fragile, tentative thoughts about what we should do next, who we should call – thoughts upon which an adequate future for us depends – for the sake of the more obvious drama of the moment. But the drama won't save us, and cares not a jot about our development or our real responsibilities.

It feels counter-intuitive to think that there might be certain things more important than the news. But there is: our own lives, which we have (troublingly) been granted such prestigious reasons and means to avoid confronting.

Normality

Most of us are rather interested in being normal. We want to belong, and worry about ways in which we don't. No matter how much we praise individualism and celebrate ourselves as unique, we are, in many areas, deeply concerned with fitting in.

It is therefore unfortunate that our picture of what is normal is often way out of line with what is actually true and widespread. Many things that we might assume to be uniquely odd or disconcertingly strange about us are in reality completely average and ubiquitous, though rarely spoken of in the reserved and cautious public sphere.

The idea of 'normal' currently in circulation is not an accurate map of what is actually customary for a human being. Each one of us is far more compulsive, anxious, sexual, high-minded, mean, generous, playful, thoughtful, dazed and at sea than we are ever encouraged to admit.

Part of the reason for our misunderstanding of our normality comes down to a basic fact about our minds: we know through immediate experience what is going on inside us, but only know about other people from what they choose to tell us, which will almost always be a very edited version of the truth.

We know what we've done at 3 a.m. but imagine others sleeping peacefully. We know our somewhat shocking desires from close up; we are left to guess about other people from what their faces tell us, which is not very much.

This asymmetry between self-knowledge and knowledge-of-others is what lies behind loneliness. We simply can't trust that our deep selves can have counterparts in those we meet, so we stay silent and isolated. The asymmetry encourages shyness too, for we struggle to believe that the imposing, competent strangers we encounter can have any of the vulnerabilities and idiocies we're so familiar with inside our own characters.

Ideally, the task of culture should be to compensate for the failings of our brains by assisting us to a more correct vision of what other people are normally like, by taking us, in a realistic but seductive way, into the inner lives of strangers. This is what novels, films and songs should constantly be doing: defining and evoking states of mind we thought we were alone in experiencing, in order to alleviate our loneliness.

We are particularly bad at recognising how normal it is to suffer and to be unhappy. Around relationships, for example, we constantly operate with an image of the bliss of others, which mocks and undermines our own efforts to keep going with flawed but eminently 'good enough' unions.

We become embarrassed, too, by our close-up knowledge of our own sexuality, which appears more perverse than that of anyone we know. It almost certainly isn't. We simply haven't been told the full story.

Our culture often tries to project an idea of an organised, poised and polished self, as the standard way most people are. We should discount any such myth. Other people are always far more likely to be as we know we are, with all our quirks, fragilities, compulsions and surprising aspects, than they are to be like the apparently 'normal' types we meet in social life.

Pessimism

A pessimist is someone who calmly assumes from the outset, and with a great deal of justification, that things tend to turn out badly in almost all areas of existence. Strange though it may sound, pessimism is one of the greatest sources of human serenity and contentment.

The reasons are legion. Relationships are rarely ever the blissful marriage of two minds and hearts that Romanticism teaches us to expect; sex is invariably an area of tension and longing; creative endeavour is pretty much always painful, compromised and slow; any job will be irksome in many of its details; children will always resent their parents, however well-intentioned and kindly the adults may try to be. Politics is evidently a process of muddle and unsatisfactory compromise.

Our satisfaction in this life is critically dependent on our expectations. The greater our hopes, the greater the risks of rage, bitterness and disappointment.

Many forces in our society conspire to stoke our hopes unfairly. Our commercial and political culture is tragically built upon the manufacture of promises of improbably beautiful scenarios. These forces tap into a natural, though profoundly mistaken, tendency of the human mind to think that the possession of hope must be the key to happiness (and kindness).

Like optimists, pessimists would like things to go well. But by recognising that many things can, and probably will, go wrong, the pessimist is adroitly placed to secure the good outcome both of these parties ultimately seek. It is the pessimist who, having never expected anything to go right, tends to end up with one or two things to smile about.

Philosophy

The best way to understand the true purpose of philosophy is to study its etymology. In ancient Greek, *philo* means love; *sophia* means wisdom. Philosophy is the grand name given to the quest to lead a wiser life.

At the start of the history of philosophy, Socrates arrived at a novel approach to wisdom. He believed that a huge amount of suffering unfolds because of our inability to use our minds correctly. We don't analyse our emotions; we can't understand our past; we respond with undue haste to certain of our feelings. We haven't begun to understand ourselves.

To this end, he pioneered the basic tools of philosophy: self-analysis, logical examination, introspection, conversation and friendship.

Socrates was the opposite of a disengaged academic: he believed that the only point of thinking was if it could be therapeutic, if it could help us to be slightly less agitated, confused and sorrowful individuals.

The aim of philosophy was – and still is – to help us cope better with our problems by introducing us to accurate and powerful ideas. Philosophy, as Socrates saw it, could be a School of Life.

Self-Sabotage

It is normal to expect that we will always actively seek out our own happiness in relationships and careers, yet we often act as if we were deliberately out to ruin our chances. When going on dates, we may lapse into unnecessarily opinionated and antagonistic behaviour. In relationships, we may drive well-intentioned partners to distraction through repeated unwarranted accusations and angry explosions. At work, we may stumble before the biggest chances.

Such behaviour can't always be put down to mere bad luck. It may deserve a stronger, more intentional term: self-sabotage. We destroy our opportunities because of a background sense that success is undeserved. This breeds a compulsion to bring our outer reality into line with our inner one, so that we end up being as unsuccessful as we feel.

Hope is hard for self-saboteurs to endure. It may feel internally easier to destroy our own happiness at a time of our own choosing, rather than to wait for circumstances to do the trick for us (as they surely will), when we are unprotected and trusting. Failing feels grim but – at least – safely grim.

Our sense of what we deserve emerges from childhood. When we carry about with us a legacy of not quite having a right to satisfaction, the good will of others may prove bewildering and inspire unconscious attempts to repel or disappoint it self-destructively. It will simply feel more normal and therefore comfortable to be disliked or ignored.

Or we may, when we were younger, have been exposed to exceptionally brutal disappointments at a time when we were too fragile to withstand them. Perhaps we hoped our parents would stay together and they didn't. Or we hoped our father would eventually come back from another country and he stayed away. Somewhere in our characters, a deep association has been forged between hope and danger, along with a corresponding preference to live quietly with disappointment, rather than more freely with hope.

The solution is to remind ourselves that we can, despite our fears, survive the loss of hope. We are no longer those who suffered the disappointments responsible for our present timidity. The conditions that forged our caution are no longer those of adult reality. The unconscious mind may be reading the present through the lenses of decades ago, but what we fear will happen has in truth already happened; we are projecting into the future a catastrophe that belongs to a past we have not had the chance to fathom and mourn adequately.

We are suffering from an enduring localised immaturity: an archaic part of us remains as it was when we were young. It has not been able to grow and shed its terrors. The intensity of fear is based on the idea that we can only bring childhood resources to the problem. We still feel the same age as when we met a horrendous loss.

But we're grown now. We have the capacity to cope very well. Should this relationship fail, should this job not work out, should our hopes not be met, we'll be sad for a while, but we won't be destroyed. We are not in as much danger as the primitive part of the mind thinks – and as we once were. The catastrophe is behind us.

If happiness has not been a big part of our history, we should be conscious of how hard or unnerving it may prove to get close to some of the things we truly want.

Tears

From early on in our lives, we are put under a great deal of pressure not to be that most terrifying and regressive of creatures, a cry baby. It's infants who cry, not parents or senior managers.

No wonder, then, that we tend to insist that we're fine, that we say we're doing well, that we're moving forward, that things are coming together.

But inside, no wonder if matters are seldom so easy. We register everything. We notice the withheld smile of a colleague we quietly despise, the silence all morning when we'd hoped for a message, the friend's promotion that throws a spotlight on our modest achievements. At the time, we laugh it off, we like to move on fast, we don't even admit the distress to ourselves, but it's all been noticed and it festers within us. It settles in a deep reservoir which is slowly filling up and is connected by a complicated hydraulic system that eventually enforces on us a heaviness of spirit, a dry smile, bitterness and envy. We too quickly forget the exact details of what wounded our spirits and then can't extract the splinters from our psyches.

In order to get the shards out of us, we should undertake a peculiar-sounding exercise. We should close our eyes and ask ourselves: what right now registers as sad? Where are we in pain?

One of the wisest things about very young children is that they have no shame or compunction about bursting into tears, because – compared with adults – they have a more accurate and less pride-filled sense of their place in the world: they know they are small beings in a hostile and unpredictable realm, that they can't control much of what is happening around them and that there is a great deal to feel confused about. Why not then, on a fairly regular basis, collapse into some highly salutary sobs at the sheer scale of the sorrow of being alive?

It's regrettable that such wisdom gets lost as we age. We start to associate maturity with invulnerability and competence. But this is the height of danger and bravado. Realising we can no longer cope is an integral part of true endurance. Moments of losing courage belong to a brave life. If we do not allow ourselves frequent occasions to bend, we will be at great risk of one day fatefully snapping.

When the impulse to cry strikes us, we should be grown-up enough to consider ceding to it. We might repair to a quiet room, pull the duvet over our heads and give way to unrestrained torrents at the horribleness of it all. No thought should be too dark anymore: we are obviously no good. It's naturally far too much. Our life is – undoubtedly – ruined. We need to touch the very bottom and make ourselves at home there; we need to give our sense of catastrophe its fullest claims.

Then, at a point in the misery, some idea – however minor – will enter our minds and make a tentative case for the other side: we'll remember that it would be pleasant to have a hot bath, that we have one or two good friends and an interesting book still to read – and we'll know that the worst of the storm is over.

In sensible households, we should all have signs, a bit like the sort they have in hotels, that we can hang on our doors and announce to passers-by that we are spending a few minutes inside doing something essential to our humanity and inherently connected to our capacity to live like a grown-up: sobbing like a lost child.

The Faulty
Walnut

The phrase 'the faulty walnut' makes affectionate reference to the instrument that sits on top of our spinal cords, an organ that is hugely powerful, inventive, nimble, capable of astonishing calculation and – at the same time – dangerously and pervasively flawed. Paradoxically, the way to greater lucidity is not to place ever deeper faith in our walnuts; it is to keep their misleading, exaggerated and deceptive nature constantly at the forefront of our thoughts. Wisdom begins with a recognition of certain of our fundamental inclinations to folly and blindness.

The walnut is marked by a range of stubborn defects that are dangerously hard to extirpate, let alone recognise in good time. It is prone to desiring and fearing without properly assessing reality. It doesn't understand its own motives or pleasures. It quickly locks onto answers and is vain and squeamish around the arduous business of self-examination. When pressed for clarification, it typically grows blank or aggressive. It is slyly expedient, preferring short-term sentimental peace to hard long-term truths. It is constantly derailed – in ways it haughtily refuses to recognise – by hormones, low sugar levels and tiredness. It doesn't readily accept its physical nature, and often petulantly resists an imperative to get an early night. It is deeply marked by its early childhood experiences in ways it can't fathom without many hours of adult introspection (which it is generally disinclined to invest in). It repeatedly transfers emotions from the past onto the present, where they don't quite belong, and thereby over- or under-reacts to situations in the here and now. It is structurally unable to count its own blessings and is overwhelmingly focused on the future. It is wired for perpetual anxiety and nagging dissatisfaction.

All the more pity then, that we inhabit an essentially Romantic culture that proclaims its awe of the power of our brains and is reverent towards their first verdicts and schemes – what we call our 'instincts'. We hear that it is good to 'trust our feelings', that reason is 'cold' and that there is a danger we might end up 'thinking too much' (rather than, as is always the case, merely thinking badly, which is a different thing).

When we follow our walnuts' instinctive promptings, our lives threaten rapidly to come undone: we don't pay sufficient attention to our biases and blind spots; we become entangled in relationships that repeat harmful childhood patterns; we pursue careers unsuited to our true yet unknown natures; we waste a lot of time on things that don't properly satisfy us …

Compensation for the flaws of our minds is the task of culture. Culture, which includes the arts, education and politics, can be in a position to counterbalance the eccentricities and foolishness of our walnuts. Culture can alert us to our flaws, make us cautious around our instincts and instil better habits of thinking and feeling. It should endlessly, and with great charm, tug us away from our first, emotional responses and guide us seductively towards wiser, more patient attitudes.

The art of living lies in knowing how, at an individual and societal level, to manage the melodramas and whims of the faulty walnuts through which we wonkily apprehend reality.

The Unconscious Mind

It took until the early 20th century for humanity to start to pay proper attention to a highly distinctive feature of the mind: that it is divided into a conscious and an unconscious part. In the former and far smaller section lies all that we have direct awareness of and can reflect on at will; while in the latter and far larger part lie the many processes and functions that constantly unfold somewhere within our craniums but which 'we' (the cognisant part of us) cannot directly register and would struggle to put into words.

The reason why a lot of what we do remains unconscious has to do with efficiency. Needing to have no active awareness of most mental processes allows us to focus on just one or two areas of concern. What we call thinking would quickly become impossible if we had to remain at all times alert to how we were breathing or achieving hormonal balance in our pituitary glands.

But there is a more ticklish, provocative thesis as to why certain things remain unconscious: because they violate our self-image, because we are too proud and sentimental to face up to who we actually are. A lot of what we strive to keep in the unconscious mind flies rather radically in the face of what we would like to be true about ourselves. In our unconscious, we might – for example – want to sleep with someone else's spouse or give up on our responsibilities to our children. Unconsciously, we may want to kill and maim, scream and hit. Were we to be fully aware of these less acceptable parts of ourselves, we might grow untenably disgusted by our natures. We remain unconscious from a sentimental wish for a comfortable, dignified existence.

The problem, as psychology sees it, is that this unknowing exacts a high price. However awkward it might be to face up to our proclivities, unconscious material is better off brought into the light than pressed down forcefully in our mental catacombs. We need to know what our sexuality really is and where our regrets genuinely lie; we have to get to know our true desires and actual frustrations. Wherever we remain ignorant, painful symptoms develop. We end up depressed because we don't know what we're sad about, we wind up anxious when we're ignorant of our real worries.

In order to try to make more of our unconscious mind, psychology recommends a range of strategies. We need a period – perhaps late in the evening or in the early morning – when we can ask ourselves simple-sounding essential questions like, 'What might be making you sad?' or 'Who might you be angry with?' It may help to write out the content of our minds in a journal or to finish sentences like: 'My mother is …' or 'I really need to …' Regular visits to a psychotherapist may additionally give our unconscious minds the encouragement they need to surrender some of their tightly held material without fear of censure or ridicule.

We can expect a genuine dividend from knowing more about how we feel about our parents' divorce or the rejection letter, our partner's departure or our childhood trauma. The more of us that can be consciously experienced in the day, the less frightened will be our nights.

Triggers

The phenomenon of being 'triggered' – though it may, at times, be applied too liberally – sits on top of a hugely important concept in psychological life which demands our respect, compassion and attention. To be triggered is, in its most basic form, to respond with intense fear to a situation in the here and now which, to other people, may seem blameless and unconcerning. One moment we are calm, the next we are catapulted into despair and terror; only minutes ago, the future looked hopeful, now only disaster seems to lie ahead.

Most of us who suffer from these episodes would very much like to better hold on to equanimity and hope. It may be important to know how to be scared or incensed when situations actually demand it. But (as the triggered person typically feels after an episode) it is also counter-productive and exhausting to be visited by powerful emotions that aren't warranted by what lies before us.

The way out of being uncontrollably triggered is to understand how the mechanism operates. The mind is triggered when it believes it recognises in the world around it a situation that it feels from memory to be highly dangerous. Our triggers are a secret guide to our histories: they tell us about things we were once very afraid of. We are triggered now by what we were devastated by then.

Even if we don't remember too much about our past, we can surmise everything we need to know from reverse engineering our triggers. If we are constantly afraid we are going to be excommunicated and mocked, this will – in some form – be exactly what happened to us at some stage long ago. If we're terrified that someone is going to over-power us and not listen to our 'no's', this is an almost sure echo of what we once experienced. The precise relation-ship between trigger and catalytic event may not always be literally equivalent; there can be some displacement along the way. But the link will be strong all the same. The trigger contains and maps onto a traumatic event.

The cure for triggering is love; patiently helping some-one to discriminate between black and white, terror and calm. The cure lies, too, in learning to work backwards from our current triggers to the dynamics that once created them. Rather than worrying yet more about the future, we should ask ourselves: What does my fear of what will happen tell me about what did happen?

To overcome our triggers is to come to navigate the present with the confidence and curiosity that should have been ours from the start. Maturity could be defined as: knowing what triggers us and why – and a commitment to patient exploration and understanding of the past.

Also available from The School of Life:

Essential Ideas: Love

**From the new pocket book series, featuring key ideas from
The School of Life exploring love.**

The School of Life has distilled its most essential lessons on love in order
to produce a pocket manual that is at once useful and entertaining. We
learn – among other things – how to pick partners more reliably, how to
avoid conflict and how to know whether a relationship is really for us.

We should cease to imagine that a satisfied love life is a chance event;
with this book in hand, it emerges as something that we can all plot for
and achieve.

Love is a skill, not an emotion; this is a guide to how we might master it.

ISBN: 978-1-916753-03-7

Essential Ideas: Serenity

**From the new pocket book series, featuring key ideas from
The School of Life exploring serenity.**

Knowing how to fight off anxiety and remain calm belong to the greatest
skills we can ever aspire to. Only with a serene state of mind are we in
any position to enjoy all the other good things in life: friendship, love,
family or work.

Here is a selection of The School of Life's finest essays on the art of
serenity. They teach us how to achieve the correct perspective on our
problems, how to understand the worst of our fears and how to surround
ourselves with the sort of people who can help us in our quest for a less
anxious existence.

We have – most of us – already spent far too long on needless worry;
here at last is a crucial guide to the less turbulent future we deserve.

ISBN: 978-1-916753-26-6

To join The School of Life community and find out more,
scan below:

The School of Life publishes a range of books on essential topics
in psychological and emotional life, including relationships,
parenting, friendship, careers and fulfilment. The aim is always to
help us to understand ourselves better and thereby to grow calmer,
less confused and more purposeful. Discover our full range of
titles, including books for children, here:
www.theschooloflife.com/books

The School of Life also offers a comprehensive therapy service,
which complements, and draws upon, our published works:
www.theschooloflife.com/therapy